Mini Stick

Mini Stick

The effective self-defense weapon on a key chain
by Cord Sander

Bibliografische Information der Deutschen Bibliothek:
Die Deutsche Bibliothek verzeichnet diese Publikation in der
Deutschen Nationalbibliografie; detaillierte bibliografische Daten
sind im Internet über http://dnb.ddb.de abrufbar.

Umschlaggestaltung, Herstellung und Verlag:
BoD – Books on Demand

ISBN: 978-3-7448-6705-4

Contents

Caution

All of the techniques described here are dangerous and can lead to severe damage. They should be carefully practiced and only used in case of emergency. The publisher, author and everyone who helped work on this book deny all liability.

Preamble

There are many forms of self-defense. The most honorable one is without question the unarmed one, as long as certain rules of morale and honor are observed. Naturally, if you are being brutally attacked in real life, honor and morale are hard to find. Still, every fighter should be aware of the consequences their actions can have and be capable of evaluating the situation carefully. Of course one's' own safety is the number one priority for me as well. But if I have an obviously inferior opponent, I have to be capable of holding onto my morale and honor in order to guarantee his health.

There are a lot of self-defense weapons on the market that are accessible with and without a license, and every single one has its pros and cons. The biggest problem is most commonly the fact that the person using the weapon has not been properly trained in how to use it. They hope to just do the right thing in a situation that is dominated by fear and stress. Statistics tell us that about 70% of people trying to defend themselves with irritant gas hit themselves and therefore are unable to fight.

There is no such thing as the perfect defense weapon for every situation and attack. The Mini Stick is not an exception. But it provides loads of possibilities as long as they are practiced and carefully used. This way the little stick becomes a very effective weapon and can be used in many situations.

Chapter 1

What is the Mini Stick?

Mini Stick – the effective self-defense weapon on a key chain

This short weapon which can be carried on a key chain at all times is excellent for self-defense. But I have seen so many people owning the Mini Stick and having no idea of all the possibilities it provides. This booklet shows a broad variety of different self-defense techniques ranging from easy to hard and harmless to dangerous.

All of the attacks depicted can be varied and combined. Examples are illustrated with pictures. You can basically "pick and mix" different techniques with the Mini Stick according to the situation you are in. It's best to practice some of the attacks shown with the corresponding defense techniques until you have mastered the Mini Stick.

There are a lot of different models and designs. Most commonly the stick is between 13 cm and 16 cm long, and is made of metal or hard plastic. But it can vary in form and color, although it is most commonly black or chrome. The stick can be either tapered or straight, the tip pointed or round. Interestingly enough, in spite of this variety the price is always similar as it rarely exceeds the 10 euro mark. This is a very reasonable price for more security in your everyday life.

Traditionally this weapon is found in many different cultures and martial arts – for example in the Japanese kubodo in the form of a yubibo or koshinobo, a 20 centimeter long stick. It can also be found in the Philippines in the form of a dulo. In America and Europe it mostly goes by the name of kubotan or kubaton.

Is it forbidden?

I'm often asked if the Mini Stick is forbidden in Germany or not. The answer is no, it is not (effective June 2006). Not too long ago I was talking to a friend of mine who is a police officer. He told me to hand in the Mini Stick if requested by a police officer but demand his name in return. After that you should lodge a complaint with the authorities and the police station. The Mini Stick will be returned to its owner shortly after.

Chapter 2

Targets on the human body

Targets on the human body

The following pressure points are just a small selection of weak points on the human body.

1. Pressure points on the front of the human body:

Fig. 1

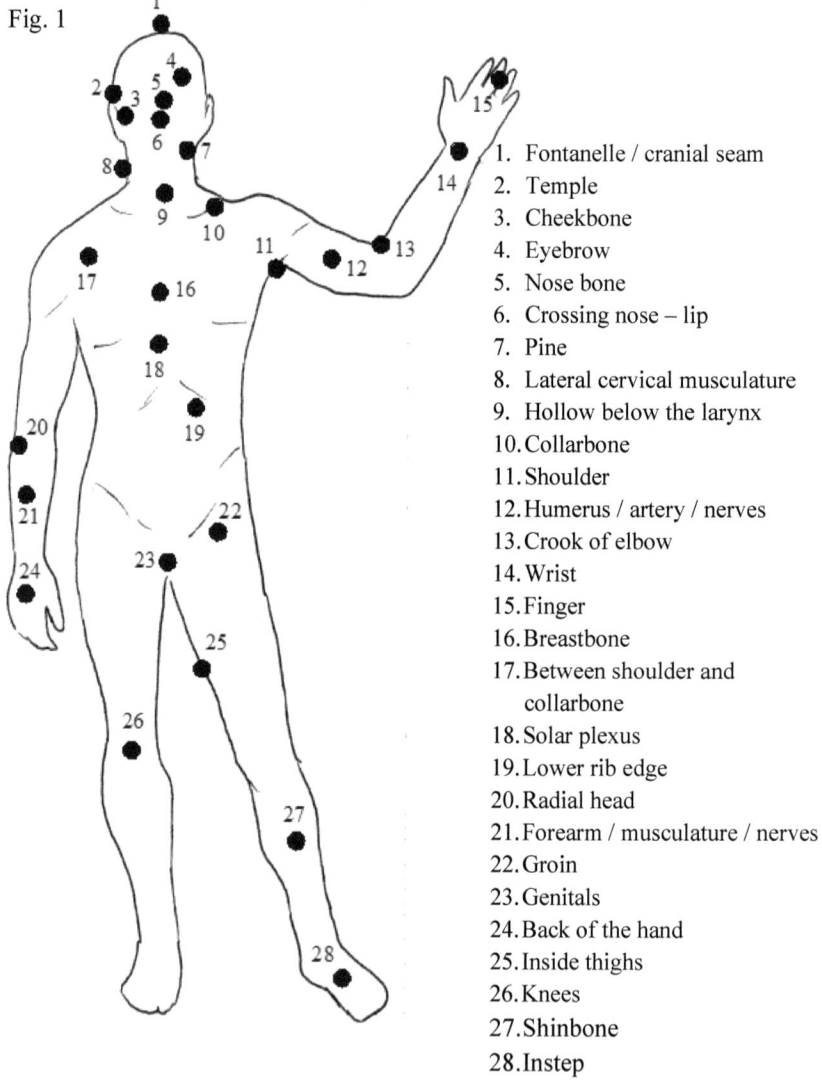

1. Fontanelle / cranial seam
2. Temple
3. Cheekbone
4. Eyebrow
5. Nose bone
6. Crossing nose – lip
7. Pine
8. Lateral cervical musculature
9. Hollow below the larynx
10. Collarbone
11. Shoulder
12. Humerus / artery / nerves
13. Crook of elbow
14. Wrist
15. Finger
16. Breastbone
17. Between shoulder and collarbone
18. Solar plexus
19. Lower rib edge
20. Radial head
21. Forearm / musculature / nerves
22. Groin
23. Genitals
24. Back of the hand
25. Inside thighs
26. Knees
27. Shinbone
28. Instep

2. Pressure points at the back

Fig. 2

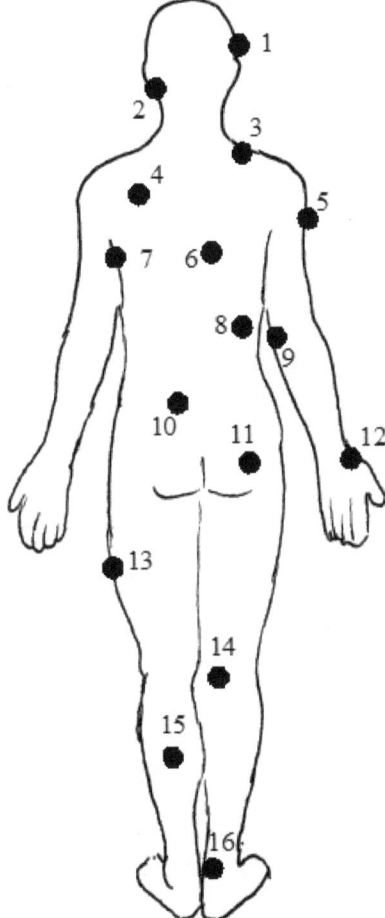

1. Temple
2. Behind the ear
3. Musculature upper shoulder
4. Scapula
5. Beginning of M. Deltoideus
6. Beginning of ribs
7. Latissimus tendon
   musculature
8. Short rib
9. Elbow
10. Coxae – sacrum
11. Bottom musculature
12. Joints of thumbs
13. Fasciae latae
14. Knee
15. Triceps surae
16. Achilles tendon

3. Pressure points on the face

Fig. 2 A

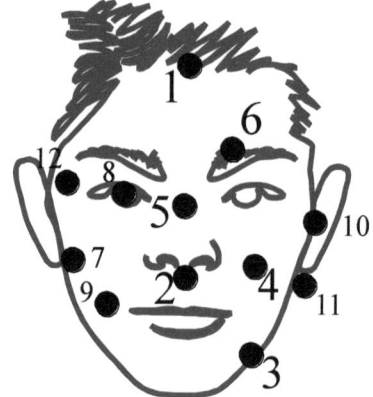

1. Fontanelle
2. Nose
3. Jaw
4. Cheekbone
5. Nose bone
6. Eyebrow
7. Mondibular joint
8. Eye
9. Cheek / tooth
10. Ear
11. Behind the ear
12. Temple

Chapter 3

Grip positions

Grip positions

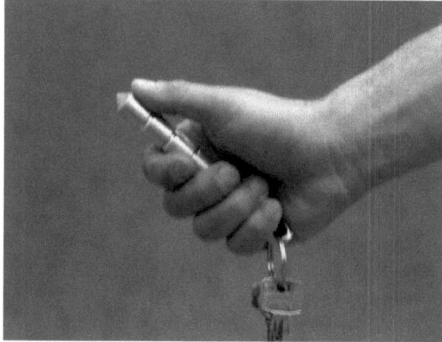

Fig. 3 – Thumb on the tip, the keys are dangling near the pinky and can be used to hit. This position is used for punches or atemi if pressure is needed.

Fig. 4 – Tip near the pinky, the keys are dangling near the thumb and can be used to strike. This grip position is good for thrusts or atemi with the tip if the arm is bent.

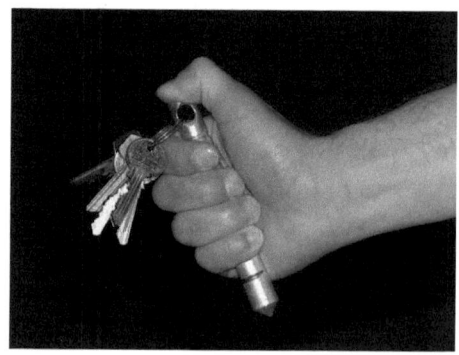

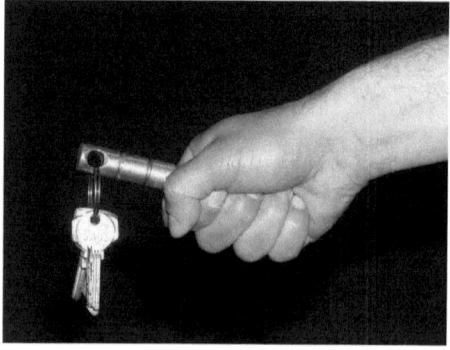

Fig. 5 – Tip securely in hand, the keys are used to strike.

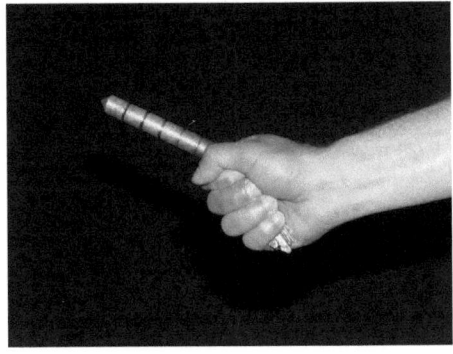

Fig. 6 – Keys in hand and the tip facing outwards. This position is good for powerful jolts with the mini stick.

Fig. 7 – Tip in left and keys in right hand.

Chapter 4

Defending yourself from being grabbed by the collar

1. Pressure on the back of the hand

Fig. 8

Fig. 9

Fig. 10

Fig. 11

The opponent grabs the collar (Fig. 8). The defender takes hold of his wrist and places the Mini Stick diagonally onto the back of the hand [second to fourth phalanx] (Fig. 9-10). The pressure on the hand bones forces the opponent to release his grasp and his hand can be pushed away (Fig. 11).

2. Continuation of 1. with subsequent finger hold

The opponent grabs the collar (Fig. 12). The defender takes hold of his wrist and places the Mini Stick diagonally onto the back of the hand (Fig. 13-14). The pressure on the hand bones forces the opponent to release his grasp and his fingers can be grabbed with both hands. The Mini Stick is positioned beneath the knuckles (Fig. 17). This finger hold should always be used with short impulses as the sensation of pain quickly subsides (Fig. 16-17).

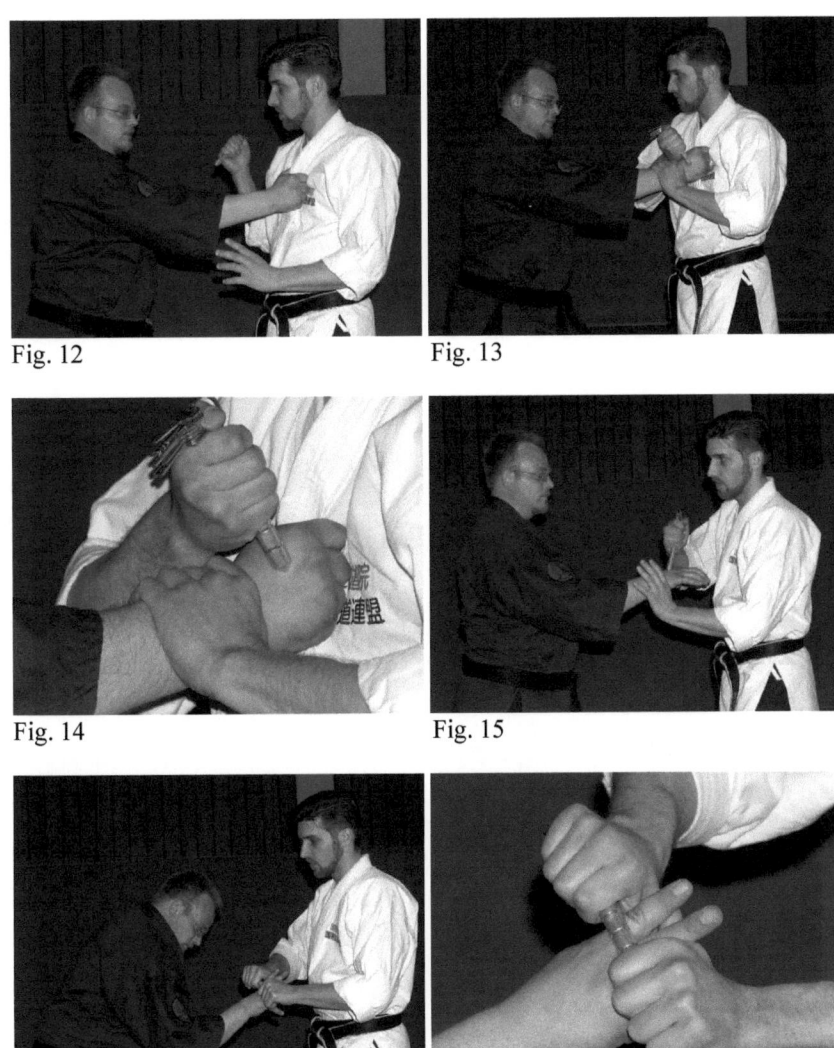

Fig. 12

Fig. 13

Fig. 14

Fig. 15

Fig. 16

Fig. 17

3. Pressure point: babysitter's elbow

Fig. 18   Fig. 19

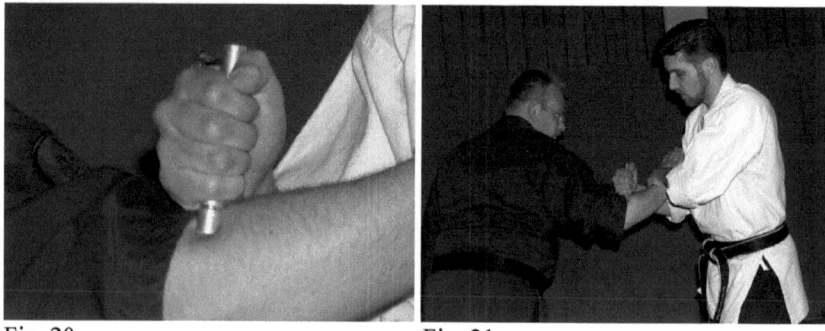

Fig. 20   Fig. 21

The opponent grabs the collar with one hand (Fig. 18). The defender grasps his hand and places the Mini Stick on the forearm (babysitter's elbow) (Fig. 19-20). The pressure applied applied forces the opponent to release his grasp and he can be pushed away (Fig. 21).

4. Inner upper arm

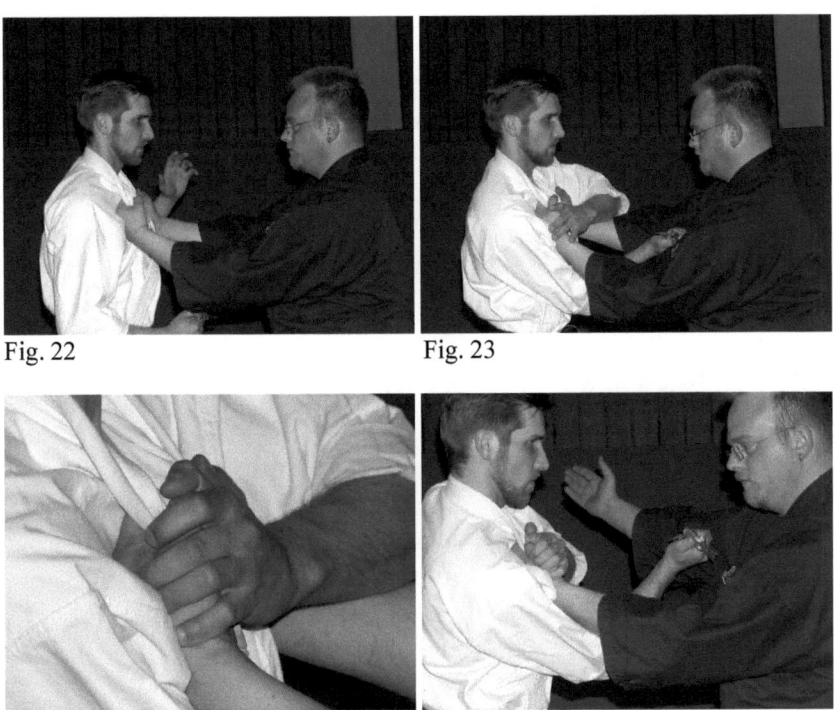

Fig. 22   Fig. 23

Fig. 24   Fig. 25

The opponent grabs the collar with one or two hands (Fig. 22). As shown above the defender holds on to them with one hand and uses the other to press the Mini Stick into the upper arm (Fig. 23-24). The opponent releases the collar because of the pressure and the defender pushes him away (Fig. 25).

5. Inner upper arm – continued

The opponent grabs the collar with one or two hands. As shown above, the defender holds on to them with one hand and uses the other to press the Mini Stick into the upper arm (Fig. 26-29). The opponent releases him because of the pressure and the defender positions the Mini Stick on the babysitter's elbow on the other arm (Fig. 30). The pressure forces the opponent down and to the left (Fig. 31). Now the defender can strike the jaw with the keys, thrust his elbow onto the attacker's head and place him in a finger hold (visible to some extent in Fig. 31).

 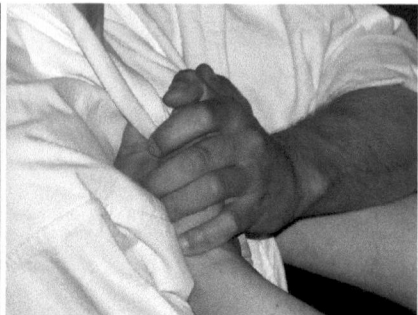

Fig. 26   Fig. 27

 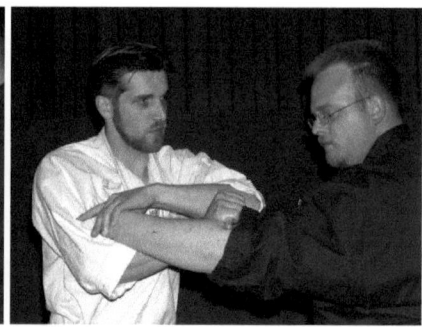

Fig. 28   Fig. 29

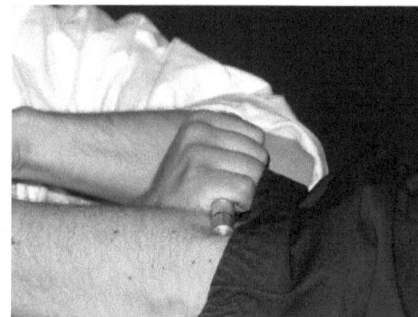 

Fig. 30   Fig. 31

6. Elbow pressure point

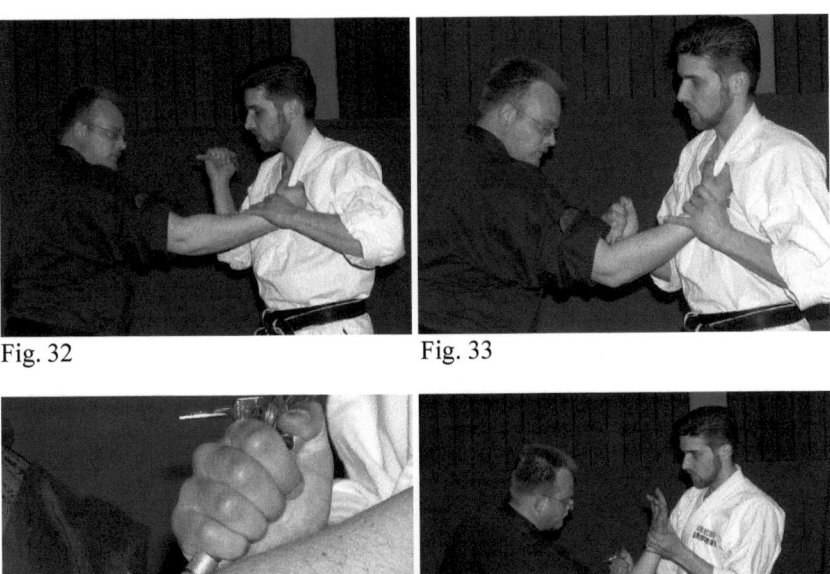

Fig. 32

Fig. 33

Fig. 34

Fig. 35

The opponent grabs the collar with one hand (Fig. 32). The defender uses his free hand to keep the attacker's hands in place while positioning the Mini Stick on the elbow (Fig. 33-34). The pressure applied applied forces the opponent to release his hold and he can be pushed backwards (Fig. 35). Afterwards a finger hold can be applied.

7. Shoulder 1

Fig. 36   Fig. 37

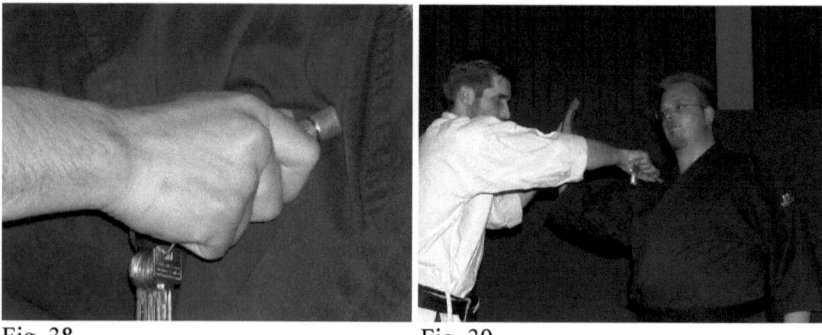

Fig. 38   Fig. 39

The opponent grabs the collar with one hand (Fig. 36). This hand is held in place and the tip of the Mini Stick is positioned in the hollow between acromion and collarbone (Fig. 37-38). The pressure applied forces the opponent to release his grip (Fig. 39) and he can be controlled with a wrist hold.

8. Shoulder II – Pressure on the supraspinatus (shoulder blade)

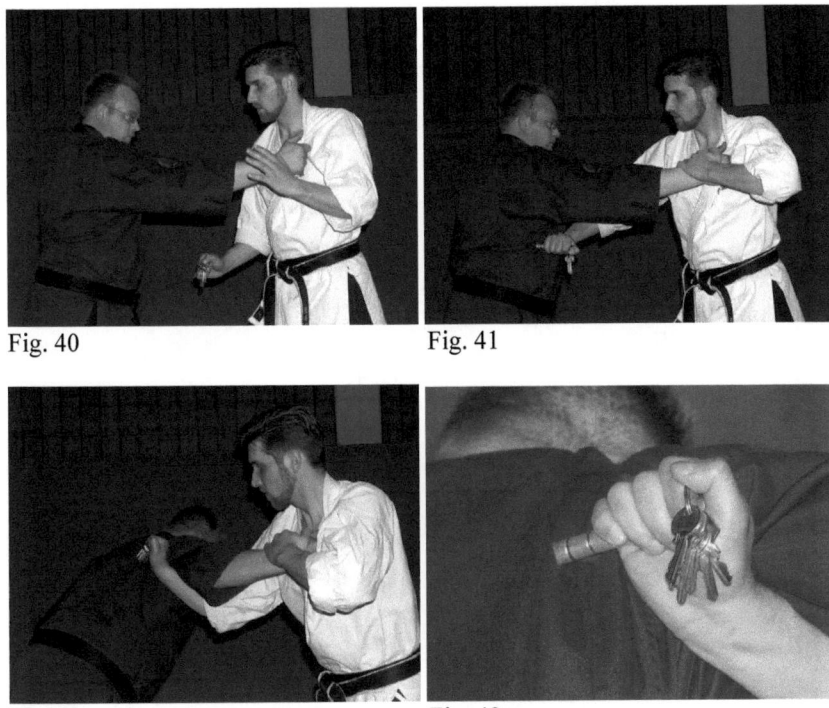

Fig. 40   Fig. 41

Fig. 42   Fig. 43

The opponent grabs the reverse of the top with one hand (Fig. 40). The defender holds his hand in place and jabs quickly into his ribs. The tip of the Mini Stick is positioned on the shoulder blade (Fig. 41-43). Use caution and exercise the next moves with great care and precision, as this moment provides the opportunity for a counterattack on one's own ribs. The defender still holds his opponent's hand in place. The pressure point of the Mini Stick is shifted through a tilting motion which forces the opponent forwards. This causes him to stumble and release his grip.

9. Shoulder II – Pressure on shoulder blades – variation

Fig. 44

Fig. 45

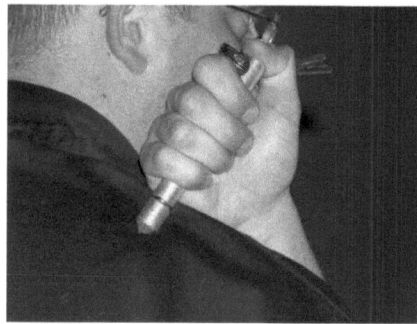

Fig. 46

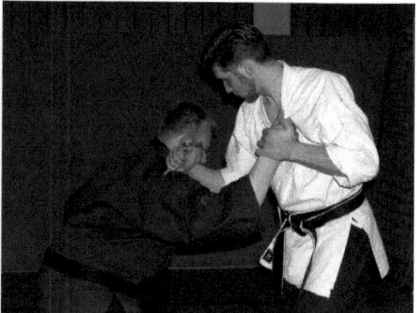

Fig. 47

Fig. 48

The opponent grabs the collar with one hand (Fig. 44). The defender holds his hand in place. The tip of the Mini Stick is positioned on the shoulder blade (Fig. 45-46). Use caution and exercise the next moves with great care and precision as this moment provides the opportunity for a counterattack on ones' own ribs. The defender still holds his opponent's hand in place. The pressure point of the Mini Stick is shifted through a tilting motion which forces the opponent onto his knees (Fig. 47). The defender releases his grip and takes a step back (Fig. 48).

10. Wrist hold

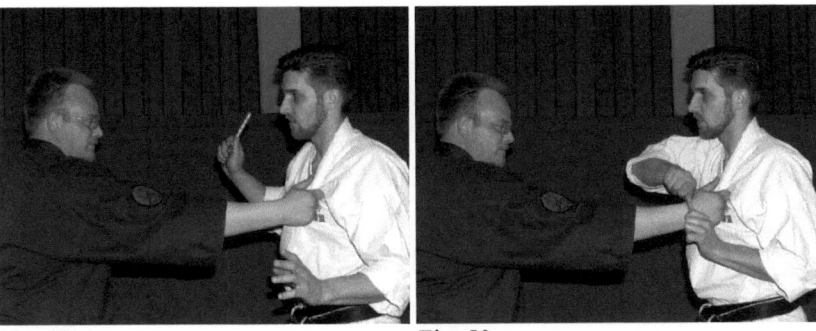

Fig. 49   Fig. 50

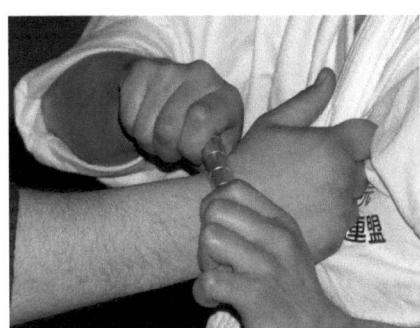

Fig. 51   Fig. 52

Fig. 53

The opponent grabs the collar with one hand (Fig. 49). The Mini Stick is placed diagonally over the wrist and held in place with the left and right hand on both ends (Fig. 50-51). The thumbs are on the palm of the hand and put pressure on the Mini Stick (Fig. 52). As soon as the defender takes one step back this joint lock takes full effect (Fig. 53). Now the opponent can be fully controlled on the ground.

11. Pressure point: larynx

Fig. 54

Fig. 55

Fig. 56

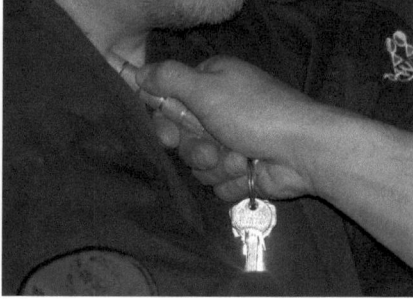

Fig. 57

Fig. 58

The opponent grabs the collar with both hands (Fig. 54). They are held in place with the defender's free hand while he hunches his shoulders to protect himself from a choke hold (Fig 55). The tip of the Mini Stick is pressed into the pressure point <u>under</u> the larynx. Caution, do not directly hit the larynx as it could be lethal (Fig. 56-57). The pressure applied forces the opponent backwards, he releases his grip and the defender takes a step back (Fig. 58).

Chapter 5

**Defenses against
punches and kicks**

1. Control hold while standing I

Fig. 59   Fig. 60

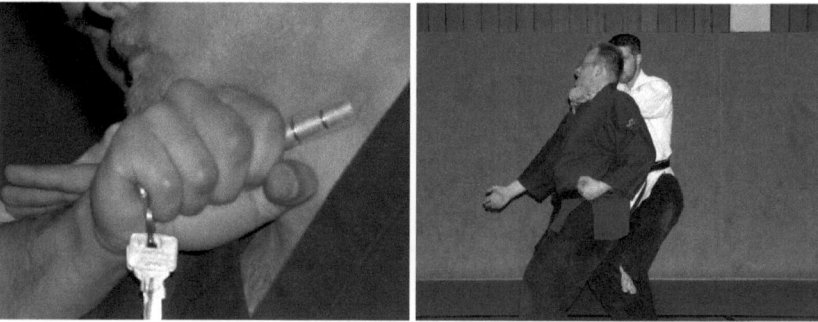

Fig. 61   Fig. 62

Fig. 63

The opponent advances with a straight punch. The defender immediately dodges to the left and redirects the enemy's punch with his right hand (Fig. 59). He is now positioned behind and to the right of the opponent and places the Mini Stick from the left at his throat. Simultaneously the defender applies pressure from the other side (Fig. 60-61). To better control the attacker he kicks into his knee and puts him in a control hold (Fig. 62-63).

2. Control hold while standing II

Fig. 64

Fig. 65

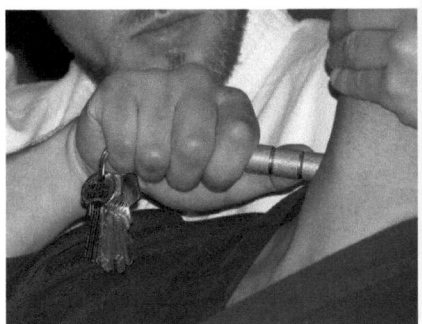
Fig. 66

Fig. 67

The opponent advances with a straight punch. The defender immediately dodges to the left and redirects the enemy's punch with his right hand (Fig. 64). He is positioned behind and to the right of the opponent and places the Mini Stick on the right side of his throat. The defender uses his free hand to pull on his enemy's chin and therefore move his head backwards, and controls his head with his forearm (Fig. 65-66). Now he pulls the attacker in a control hold backwards (Fig. 67).

3. Control hold while standing III

Fig. 68

Fig. 69

Fig. 70

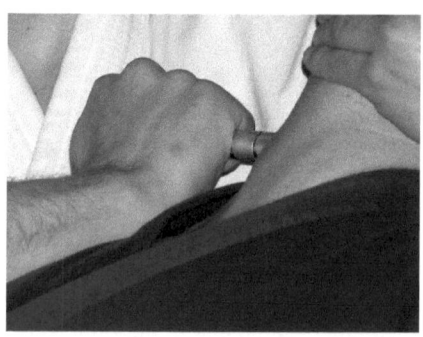

The opponent advances with a straight punch. The defender immediately dodges to the left and redirects the enemy's punch with his right hand (Fig. 68). He is positioned behind and to the right of the opponent and places the Mini Stick on the right side of his throat, immediately applying pressure. The defender uses his free hand to pull on his enemy's chin and therefore move his head backwards, and controls his head with his forearm from the other side (Fig. 69-70). As opposed to the technique shown on page 28 the Mini Stick is held in the grip position two. Now the defender pulls his attacker backwards (as shown in 1 and 2) and can bring him down to the ground if desired.

4. Direct defense I

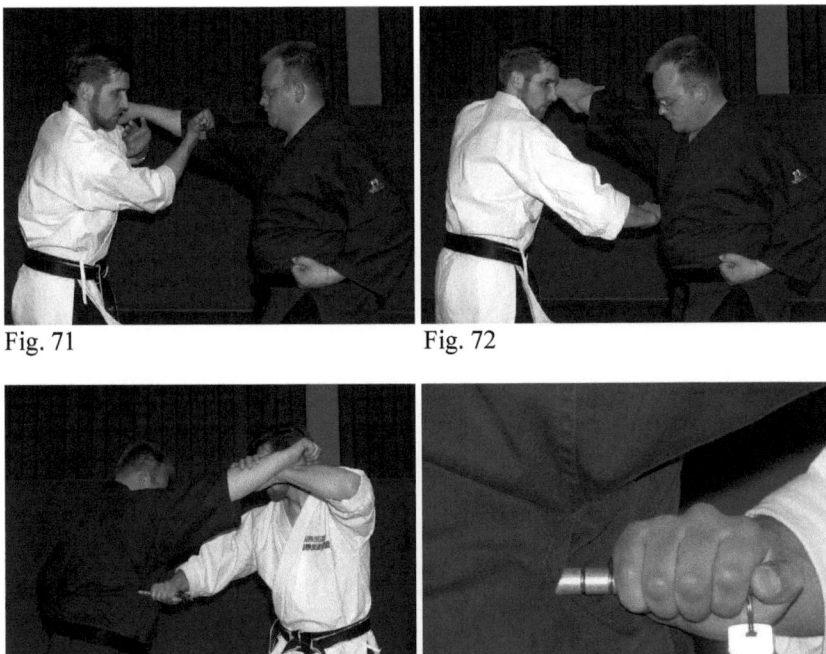

Fig. 71   Fig. 72

Fig. 73   Fig. 74

The opponent advances with a straight punch. The defender immediately dodges to the right and redirects the enemy's punch with his right hand (Fig. 71). His left hand now holds the attacking hand in place while jabbing the Mini Stick into his opponent's ribs with his right (Fig. 72-74).

5. Direct defense II

Fig. 75

Fig. 76

Fig. 77

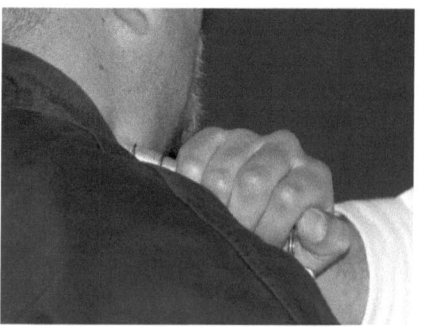

The opponent advances with a straight punch. The defender immediately dodges to the right and redirects the enemy's punch with his right hand (Fig 75). His left hand now holds the attacking hand in place while jabbing the Mini Stick into his opponent's throat with his right (Fig. 76-77).

6. Direct defense III

Fig. 78

Fig. 79

Fig. 80

The opponent advances with a straight kick. The defender immediately dodges to the front and blocks with both hands. The Mini Stick is held in the right hand and jabbed with the tip first into the attacker's upper thigh (Fig. 78-79). The right hand is rotated and the tip of the Mini Stick is thrust into his genitals (Fig. 80).

7. Direct defense IV

Fig. 81   Fig. 82

The opponent advances with a straight kick. The defender dodges to the front and secures his body with his left hand while jabbing the Mini Stick tip first into the opponent's shin with his right (Fig. 81-82).

8. Direct defense V

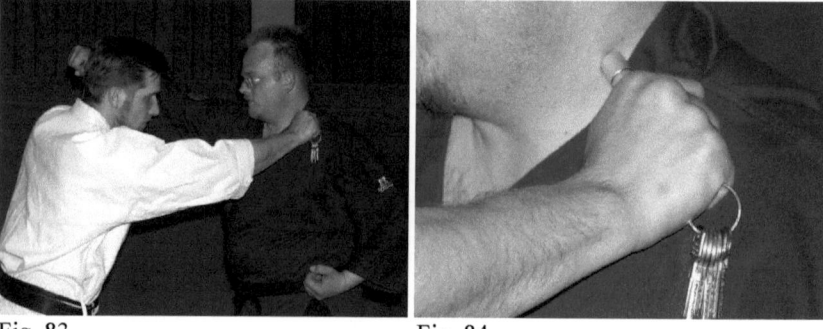

Fig. 83   Fig. 84

The opponent advances with a straight punch. The defender immediately dodges to the front and blocks the blow with his left arm. Then he jabs the Mini Stick in a semicircular motion into the throat of his opponent (Fig. 83-84).

9. Direct defense VI

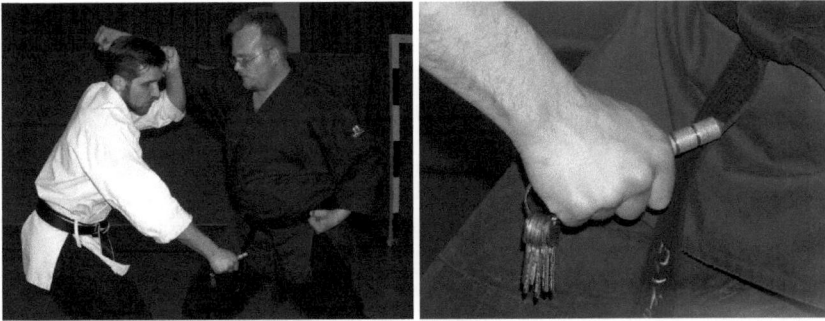

Fig. 85   Fig. 86

The opponent advances with a punch. The defender dodges to the front and blocks the blow with his left arm. Then he jabs the Mini Stick into his opponent's genitals from below (Fig. 85-86).

10. Direct defense VII

Fig. 87   Fig. 88

The opponent advances with a punch. The defender dodges to the front and blocks the blow with his left arm. The he jabs the Mini Stick into the sternum of his attacker (Fig. 87-88).

11. Direct defense VIII

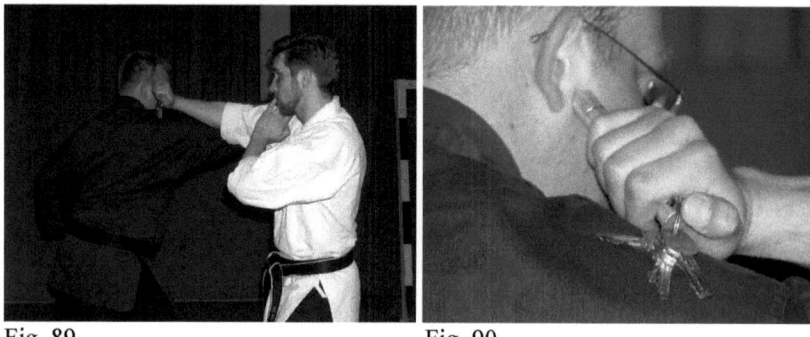

Fig. 89   Fig. 90

The opponent advances with a punch. Immediately the defender dodges to the front and shoves the Mini Stick into the attacker's jaw joint (Fig. 89-90).

12. Direct defense IX

Fig. 91   Fig. 92

The opponent advances with a low kick. Moving forward, the defender jabs the Mini Stick into his attacker's knee. As the opponent hunches over in pain the defender strikes him on the head with his keys (Fig. 91-92)

13. Direct defense X

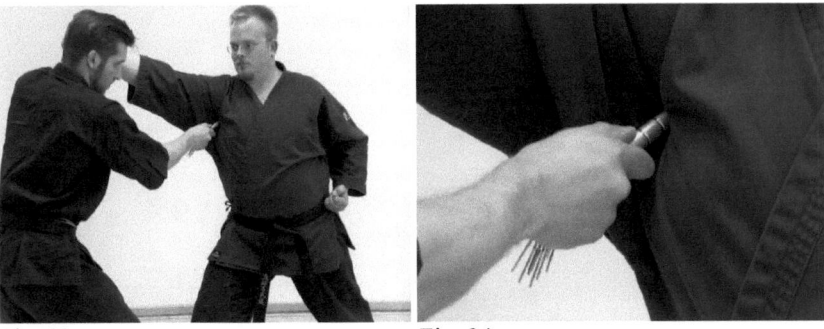

Fig. 93   Fig. 94

The opponent advances with a straight punch. The defender dodges to the front and jabs the Mini Stick into the attacker's armpit (Fig. 93-94).

14. Direct defense XI

Fig. 95

The opponent advances with a straight punch. The defender dodges to the front and hits the attacker's head with his keys (Fig. 95).

15. Direct defense XII

Fig. 96

Fig. 97

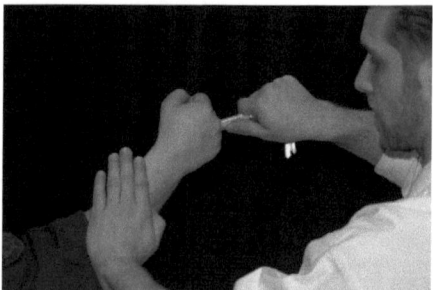

Fig. 98

The opponent advances with a punch to the face (Fig. 96-97). The defender quickly dodges to the left and redirects the punch with his left arm. He simultaneously jabs the tip of the Mini Stick into his attacker's knuckles (Fig. 98).

16. Direct defense / blow to the neck

Fig. 99   Fig. 100

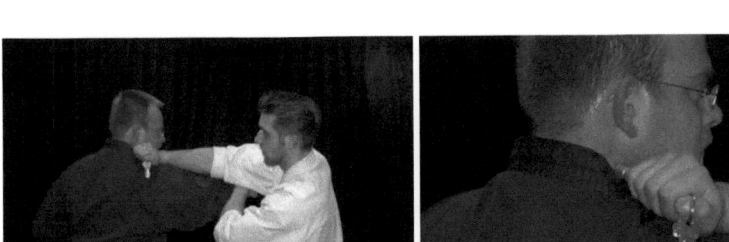

Fig. 101   Fig. 102

The attacker advances with a straight punch to the defender's face. The defender dodges diagonally to the left and redirects the punch with his left hand while positioning the Mini Stick in front of his own left shoulder (Fig. 99-100). Now the defender powerfully thrusts the Mini Stick into his attacker's neck (Fig. 101-102).

17. Direct defense / blow to the temple

Fig. 103   Fig. 104

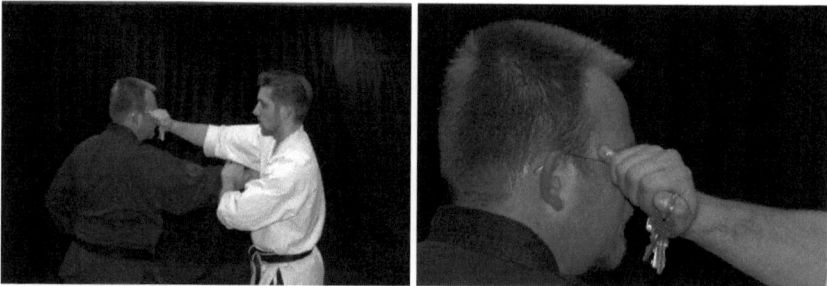

Fig. 105   Fig. 106

The attacker advances with a straight punch to the defender's face. The defender dodges diagonally to the left and redirects the punch with his left hand while positioning the Mini Stick in front of his own left shoulder (Fig. 103-104). Now the defender powerfully thrusts the Mini Stick into his attacker's temple (Fig. 105-106).

Chapter 6

Defending yourself from body locks and holds

1. From the front beneath the arms

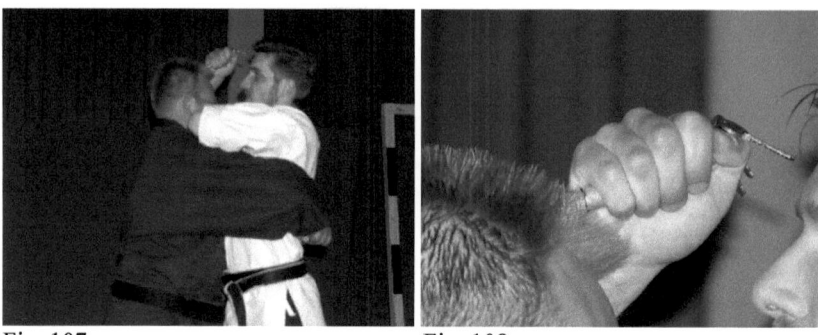

Fig. 107   Fig. 108

The opponent holds the defender in a body lock beneath his arms from the front. The defender positions the Mini Stick on the fontanelle and applies pressure on the cranial suture (Fig. 107-108). Caution: do not thrust or jab the stick, just apply pressure!

2. From the front above the arms

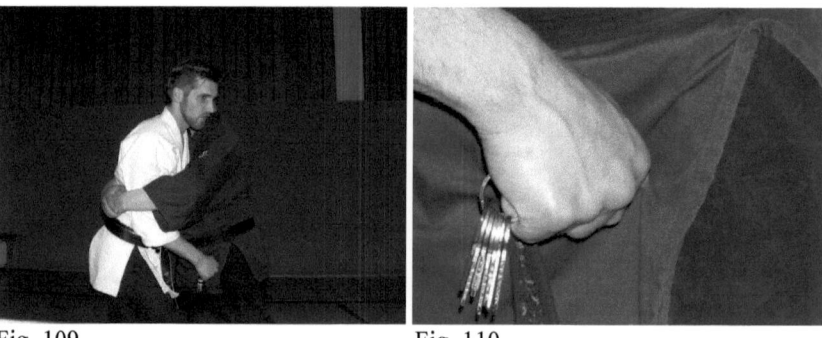

Fig. 109   Fig. 110

The opponent holds the defender in a body lock above his arms from the front. The defender positions the Mini Stick on his attacker's groin and applies pressure (Fig. 109-110) so he can be pushed away.

3. From the front above the arms – continued

Fig. 111

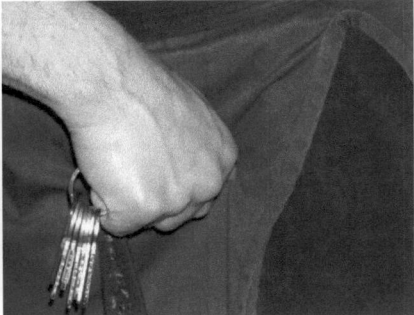

Fig. 112

Fig. 113

Fig. 114

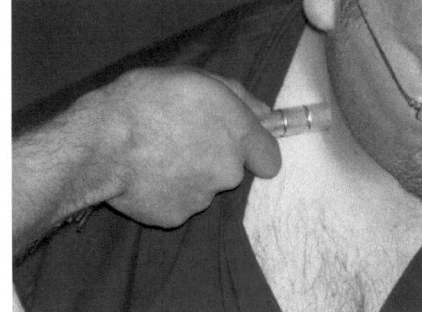

Fig. 115

The opponent holds the defender in a body lock above his arms from the front. The defender positions the Mini Stick on his attacker's groin and applies pressure (Fig. 111-112). As the opponent moves backwards the defender bursts out of the lock by spreading his arms (Fig. 113). To create distance he pushes the Mini Stick into his attacker's neck (Fig. 114-115).

4. From the back above the arms

Fig. 116

Fig. 117

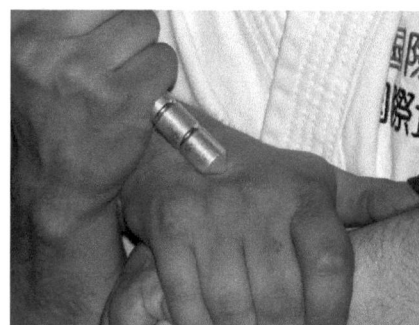

Fig. 118

Fig. 119

Fig. 120

The opponent holds the defender in a body lock above his arms from the back (Fig. 116). The defender positions the Mini Stick on the back of his opponent's hand and applies pressure between the knuckles (Fig. 117-118). As soon as the defender is released he applies pressure with the tip of the Mini Stick onto the sternum of his attacker (Fig. 119-120).

5. Headlock

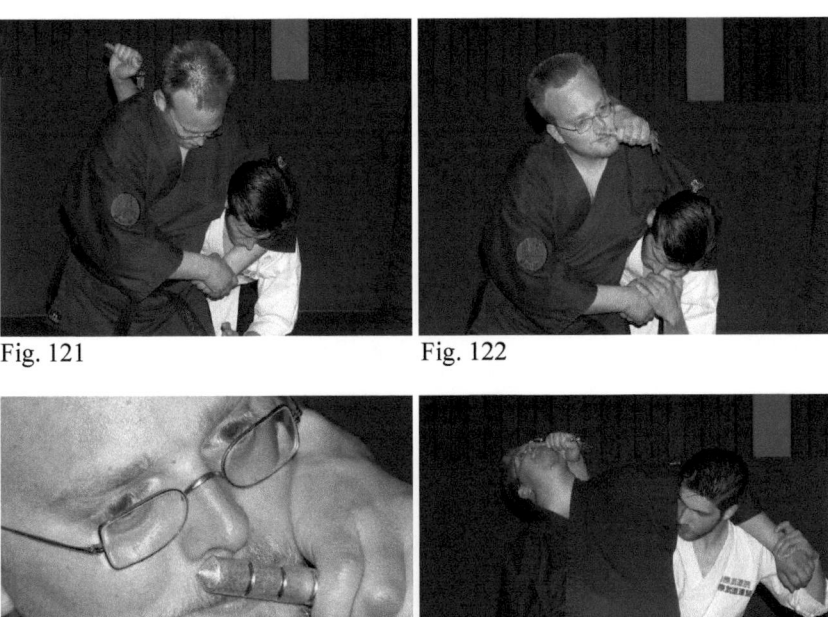

Fig. 121   Fig. 122

Fig. 123   Fig. 124

The attacker puts the defender into a headlock (Fig. 121). The defender puts his arm over his opponent's shoulder and positions the Mini Stick beneath the nose (Fig. 122-123). He applies pressure and the leverage created forces the opponent backwards, which makes it easy to bring him to the ground (Fig. 124).

6. From behind underneath the arms

Fig. 125   Fig. 126

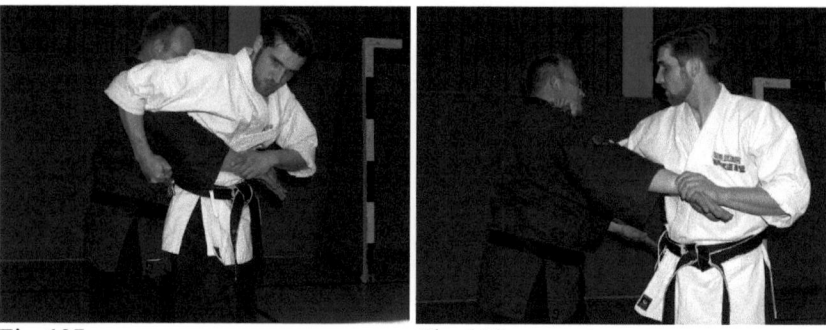

Fig. 127   Fig. 128

The defender is attacked and put in a body lock from behind, being held beneath his arms and lifted upwards (Fig. 125). He uses the Mini Stick to jab at his opponent's head (Fig. 126) and then immediately strikes into his ribs (Fig. 127). The defender is released from the hold and lands on his feet. He turns around and jabs into his attacker's neck (Fig. 128).

Chapter 7

Defenses against choke holds

1. Defense against choke holds with both hands from the front

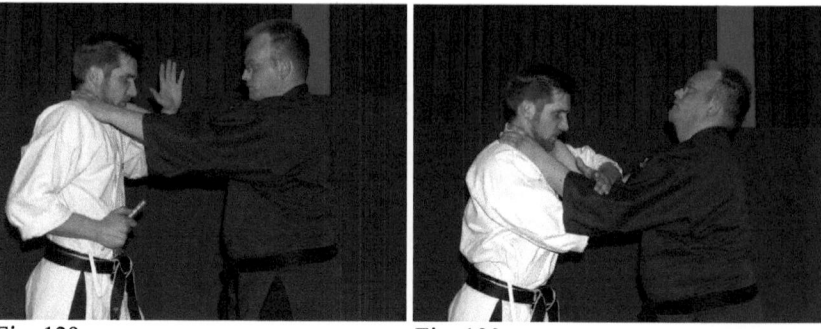

Fig. 129   Fig. 130

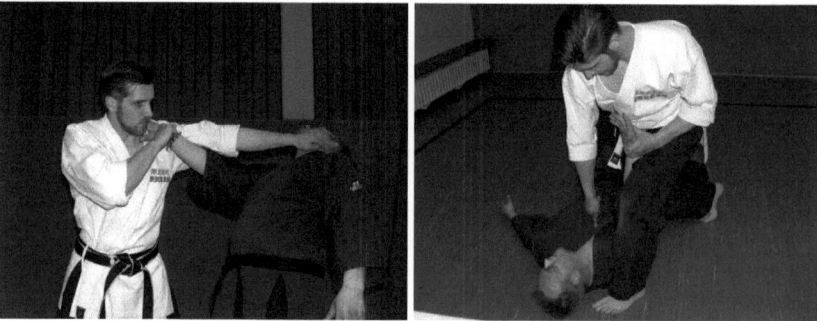

Fig. 131   Fig. 132

The attacker chokes the defender with both hands from the front. The defender pulls up his shoulders and punches into his attacker's armpit (Fig. 129). Now he thrusts the Mini Stick into the pressure point beneath the larynx (Fig. 130). He quickly changes the position of his hands. The hand that was under the attacker's armpit moves up to the chin and the other hand that is holding the Mini Stick moves down to the right wrist (Fig. 131). The defender builds up pressure by moving his left hand to the left and securing his opponent's hand with the Mini Stick on the chest (Fig. 131). This way the attacker is brought to the ground and can be controlled by applying pressure with the Mini Stick onto the sternum (Fig. 132).

2. Defense against choke hold and punch

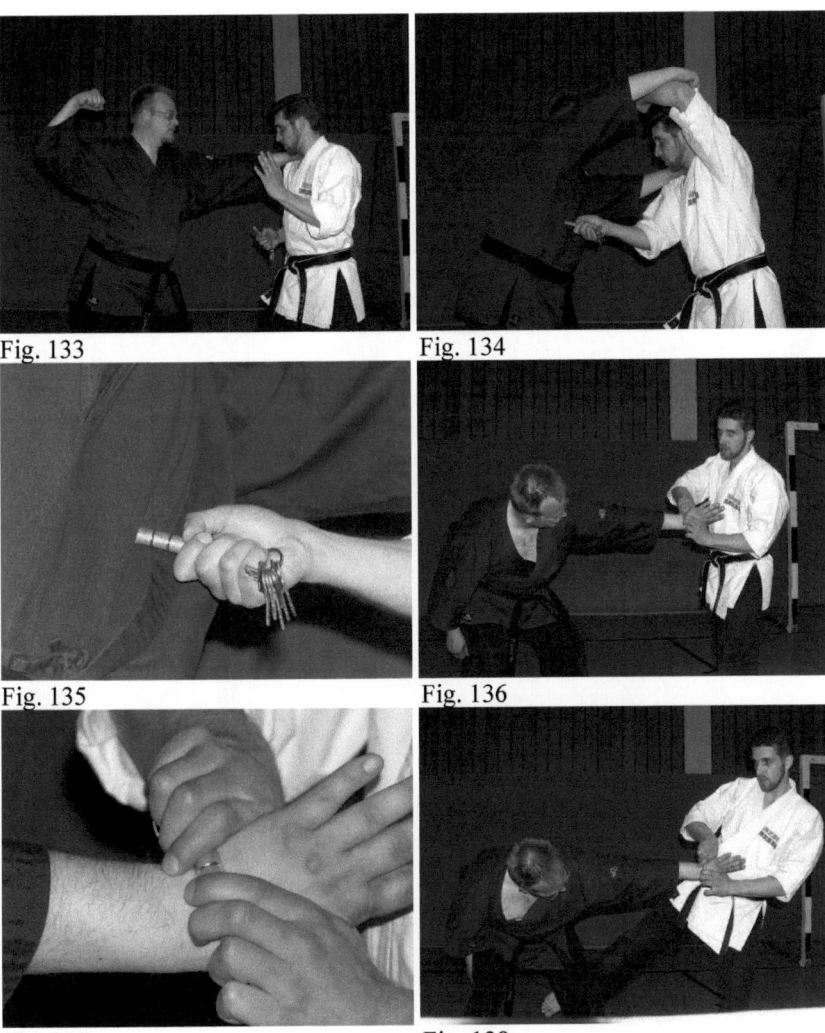

Fig. 133

Fig. 134

Fig. 135

Fig. 136

Fig. 137

Fig. 138

The attacker grabs the neck with his left hand and chokes while preparing to punch with his right (Fig. 133). The blow is blocked with the left arm while simultaneously jabbing the Mini Stick into the lower ribs (Fig. 134-135). The defender places the weapon over the attacker's hand and holds it in place with both hands (Fig. 136-137). A hand hold and a kick into the knee brings the opponent to the ground (Fig. 138).

3. Defense against choke hold and punch II

Fig. 139

Fig. 140

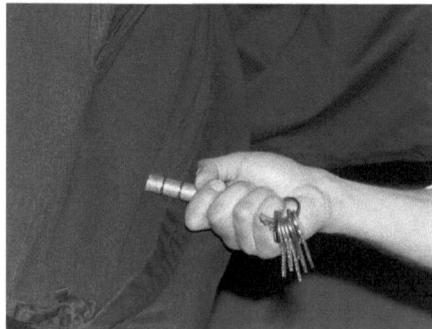
Fig. 141

Fig. 142

The opponent grabs the throat of the defender with his left hand and chokes him while preparing to punch with his right (Fig. 139). The blow is blocked with the defender's left hand as he thrusts the Mini Stick into the lower ribs of his attacker (Fig. 140-141). Then he reaches over his opponent's arm and jabs the stick into his neck (Fig. 142).

4. Defense against choke hold from the side I

Fig. 143

Fig. 144

Fig. 145

The opponent chokes with both hands from the side. The first thing the defender should do (as is recommended for any kind of choke hold attack) is to protect the neck by tucking his chin in (Fig. 143). The defender is holding the Mini Stick like a dagger (see Chapter 3, grip positions) and thrusts the tip into the ribs of his attacker (Fig. 144). Now he grabs the wrist and then jabs the keys of the Mini Stick into the elbow from below while placing the opponent in a hand hold (Fig. 145).

4a. Defense against choke hold from the side II

Fig. 146

Fig. 147

Fig. 148

Fig. 149

The opponent chokes with both hands from the side. The first thing the defender should do (as is recommended for any kind of choke hold attack) is to protect the neck by tucking his chin in (Fig. 146). Holding the Mini Stick like a dagger, the defender jabs the tip into his attacker's genitals (Fig. 147) while grabbing the wrist. The defender pulls the Mini Stick back and places the tip in the crook of the arm. The combination of the pressure applied and the hand hold makes the attacker fall to the ground (Fig. 148). Now the defender jabs the keys into the temple of his opponent (Fig. 149).

5. Defense against choke hold from behind

Fig. 150

Fig. 151

Fig. 152

The attacker chokes the defender with his forearm from behind (Fig. 150). The tip of the Mini Stick is near the thumb. The defender jabs the stick backwards into the head of his attacker (Fig. 151). Then he thrusts the stick into the forearm and frees himself with his other hand from the choke hold (Fig. 152).

6. Defense against choke hold from behind – continued

Fig. 153

Fig. 154

Fig. 155

Fig. 156

Fig. 157

Fig. 158

Fig. 159

The attacker chokes the defender with his forearm from behind (Fig. 153). The tip of the Mini Stick is near the thumb. The defender jabs the stick backwards into the head of his attacker (Fig. 154). Then he thrusts the stick into the forearm and grabs the wrist with his free hand (Fig. 155). Now the defender turns right to free himself, presses the Mini Stick into his attacker's elbow and places him in an arm hold (Fig. 156-159). It is essential that the defender keeps his attacker's hand close to his own hip to be able to keep control and apply pressure when needed. To better demonstrate the technique in the photos, this cannot be seen in Fig. 159. But Fig. 158 clearly shows how to control your opponent.

7. Defense against choke hold from the front

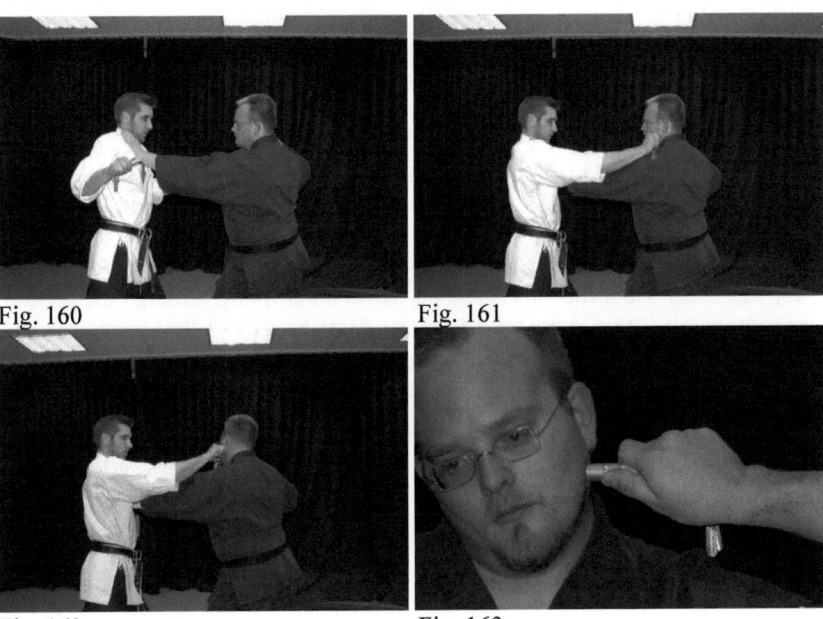

Fig. 160

Fig. 161

Fig. 162

Fig. 163

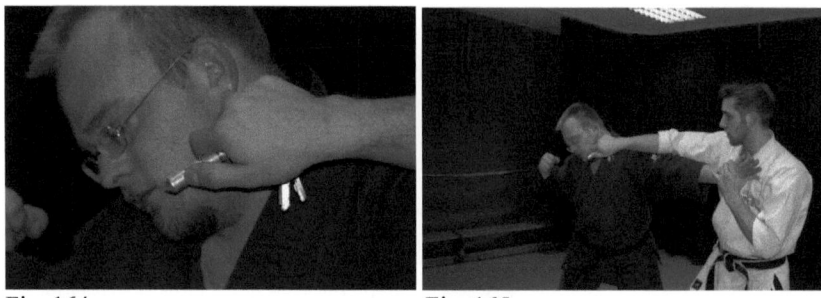

Fig. 164   Fig. 165

Fig. 166   Fig. 167

The attacker chokes the larynx with his left hand and prepares to punch with his right fist (Fig. 160). At this moment the defender tucks his chin in to protect his neck and grabs the attacker's wrist with his left hand. Then the defender uses the tip of the Mini Stick and jabs it into the jaw of his opponent, forcing him to turn to the right (Fig. 161-164). The attacking left hand of the opponent is stretched out (Fig. 165). Now the attacker is placed in an arm hold through the pressure applied on the elbow with the tip of the Mini Stick and the defender's own elbow placed on the shoulder blade (Fig. 166-167).

Chapter 8

Freeing the wrist

1. Freeing the wrist I

Fig. 168

Fig. 169

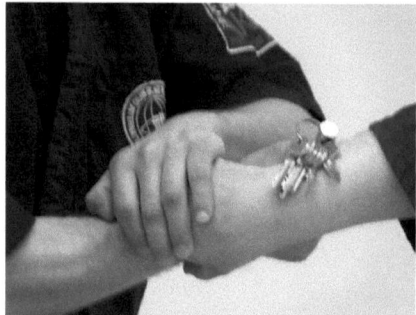
Fig. 170

Fig. 171

The attacker diagonally grabs the wrist of the defender (Fig. 168). The Mini Stick is held in hand with the keys near the thumb (as shown in the chapter on grip positions, Fig. 5). The defender uses his free hand to keep the opponent's hand in place and twists it downwards and around. Then the Mini Stick is positioned with the keys on the wrist of the opponent (Fig. 169-170). Now the attacker's arm is bent into a Z position. By applying light pressure the defender can push the hand against the opponent's collar bone and so gains control of the situation (Fig. 171).

2. Freeing the wrist II

Fig. 172

Fig. 173

Fig. 174

The wrist of the defender is grabbed with one hand. The Mini Stick is held in hand with the tip near the thumb (Fig. 172). The tip of the Mini Stick is placed on the inner forearm of the opponent (Fig. 173). To release his attacker's grip he strongly pushes the forearm down (Fig. 174). The defender controls his opponent by placing his left hand on his attacker's head as shown in the last picture. Now he has loads of possibilities for counterattacks.

3. Freeing the wrist III

Fig. 175

Fig. 176

Fig. 177

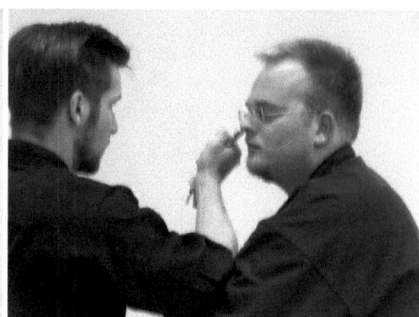

Fig. 178

The opponent grabs the wrist of the defender while preparing to punch him with the other hand (Fig. 175). The defender raises his right elbow and twists it to get the grabbed hand free. Then he shoves the Mini Stick tip first into the arm that is taking a swing at him. While doing so the defender dodges to the right (Fig. 176-177). Now he uses his free hand to block the attacker's left hand and then shoves the Mini Stick into his head (Fig. 178).

4. Freeing the wrist IV – with arm hold

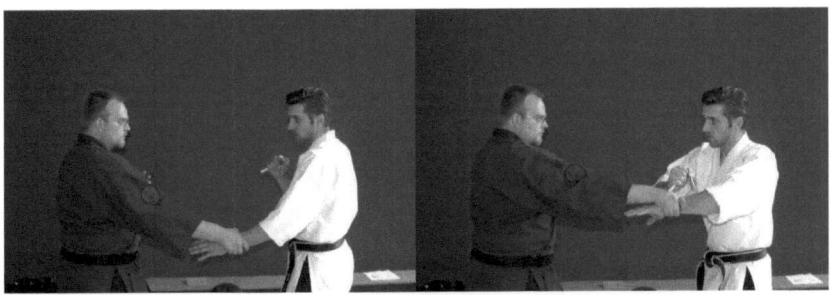

Fig. 179   Fig. 180

Fig. 181   Fig. 182

Fig. 183

The opponent grabs the defender's left hand with his right (Fig. 179). The defender immediately twists his arm up in a semicircle while placing the Mini Stick tip first onto the back of the hand. Then he grabs the opponent's right wrist (Fig. 180-181). As the defender continues this movement the attacker's arm is outstretched (Fig. 182). The opponent is placed in an arm hold by the defender through applying pressure onto the elbow while stretching the arm and pressing the Mini Stick into the back of the hand (Fig. 183).

5. Freeing the wrist V – arm tackle

Fig. 184   Fig. 185

Fig. 186   Fig. 187

![Fig. 188]

Fig. 188

The opponent grabs the wrist of the defender diagonally (Fig. 184). The defender holds the Mini Stick with the keys in his hand and then quickly hurls it under the attacker's hand and grabs it from the top with his second hand (Fig. 185). This way the opponent's hand is clamped between the defender's hands and the Mini Stick (Fig. 186). By softly pulling downwards the opponent is brought into an arm tackle (Fig. 187). This allows the defender to strike his knee up into the face of his attacker (Fig. 188).

6. Freeing the wrist VI – arm tackle

Fig. 189   Fig. 190

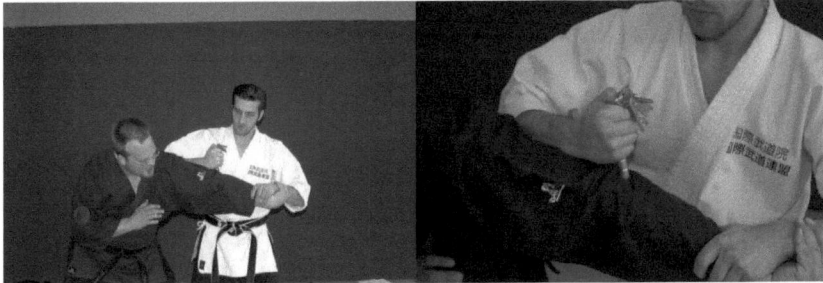

Fig. 191   Fig. 192

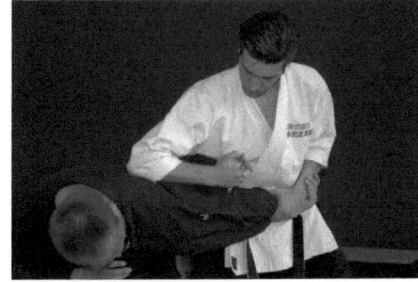

Fig. 193

The opponent diagonally grabs the defender's wrist, who holds the Mini Stick in the other hand (Fig. 189). Then the defender twists his hand upwards, allowing him in turn to grab the opponent's hand. At the same time he positions the Mini Stick on the elbow (Fig. 190-192). Now, by applying strong pressure, the attacker can easily be controlled (Fig. 193).

7. Freeing the wrist VII

Fig. 194   Fig. 195

Fig. 196   Fig. 197

The opponent grabs the wrist of the defender from the side (Fig. 194) while trying to get hold of his collar or hair. Now the defender raises his gripped hand to block the other hand of his attacker (Fig. 195). He jabs the tip of the Mini Stick into the ribs (Fig. 196) and then into the neck of his opponent (Fig. 197).

8. Freeing the wrist VIII

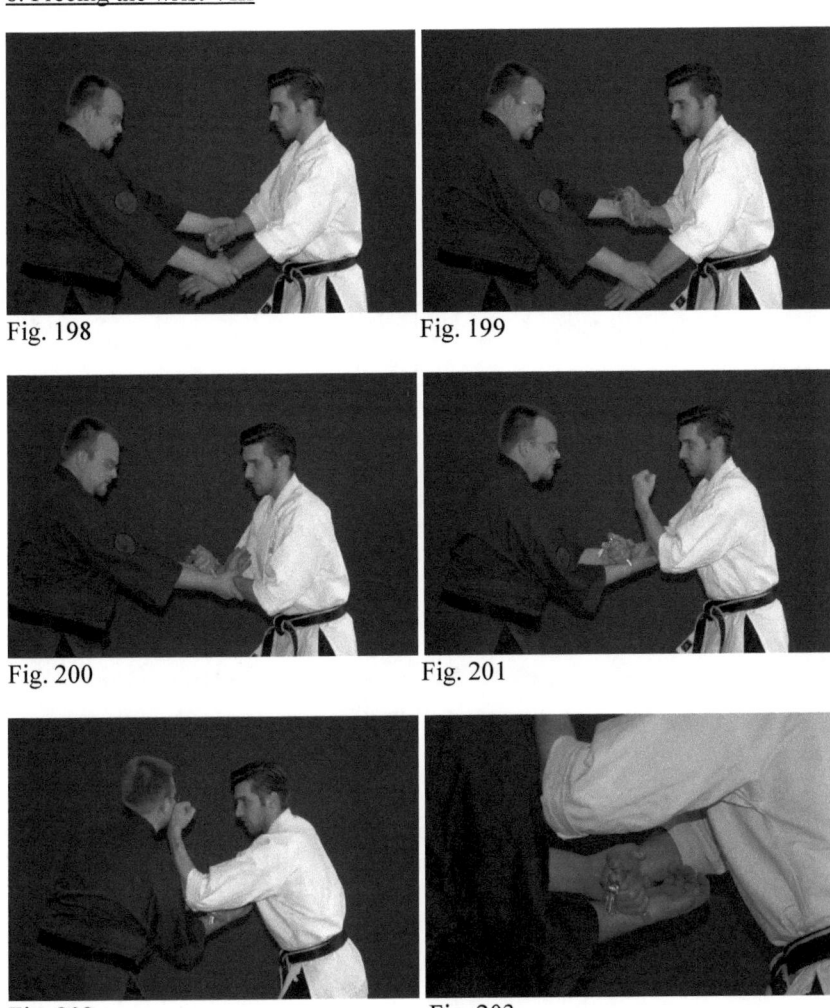

Fig. 198 Fig. 199

Fig. 200 Fig. 201

Fig. 202 Fig. 203

Both wrists are grabbed from the front (Fig. 198). The defender turns the hand holding the Mini Stick upwards (Fig. 199) and places the tip onto the wrist (Fig. 200). This allows him to free himself of the opponent's hold, and then he takes a swing at the attacker (Fig. 201-202). Now the defender has temporary control over his attacker until he frees his hold completely (Fig. 203).

9. Freeing the wrist IX

Fig. 204

Fig. 205

Fig. 206

Fig. 207

Fig. 208

Both wrists are grabbed from the front (Fig. 204). The defender turns both his right and left arm to the right and up (Fig. 205). Now the Mini Stick is placed tip first onto the wrist of the attacker while the free hand grabs that same wrist and twists it inwards (Fig. 206 – 207). Now the Mini Stick is positioned between the lower arm bones. By applying pressure on the elbow of the opponent, the defender puts him in a shoulder lock (Fig. 208).

Chapter 9

Techniques on the ground

1. Defense against choke holds on the back

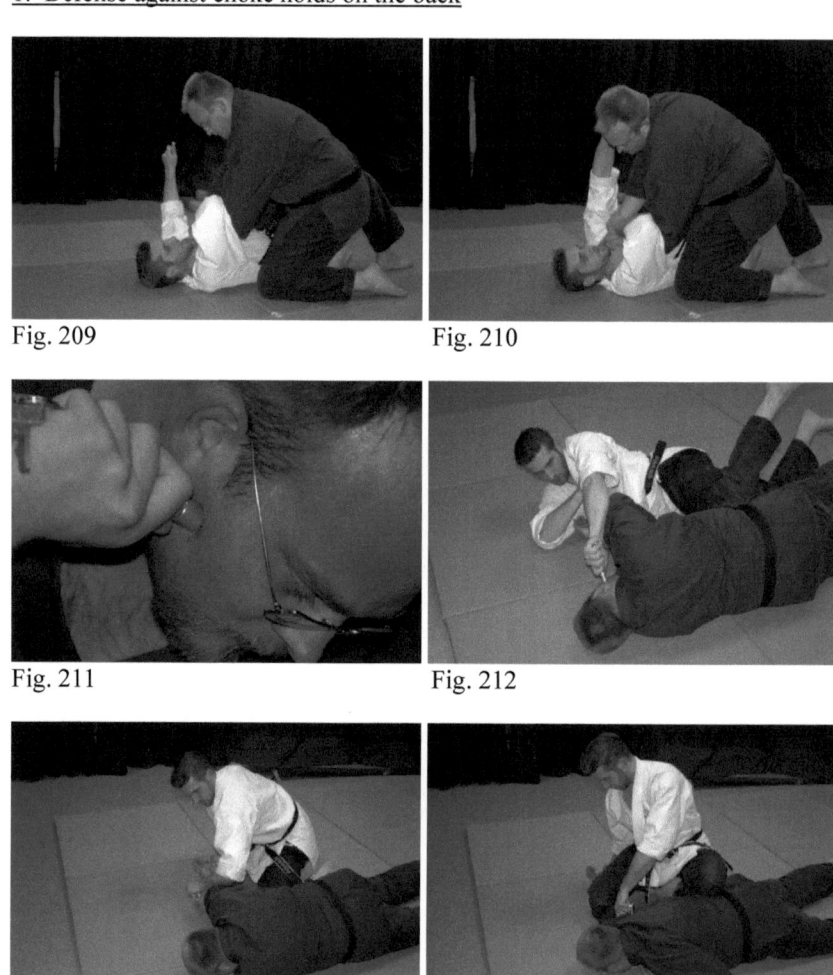

Fig. 209

Fig. 210

Fig. 211

Fig. 212

Fig. 213

Fig. 214

The attacker chokes the defender, who is lying on the ground, with both hands. First the defender tucks in his chin, then he reaches over his left arm and grabs his attacker's right wrist while thrusting the Mini Stick into his jaw (Fig. 209-211). The defender yanks up his knee into the opponent's ribs which makes him fall off to the side (Fig. 212). By placing him in an arm hold and putting pressure onto his shoulder blades, the defender gains control over the attacker and can keep him on the ground (Fig. 213-214).

2. Defense against choke holds from the back while sitting

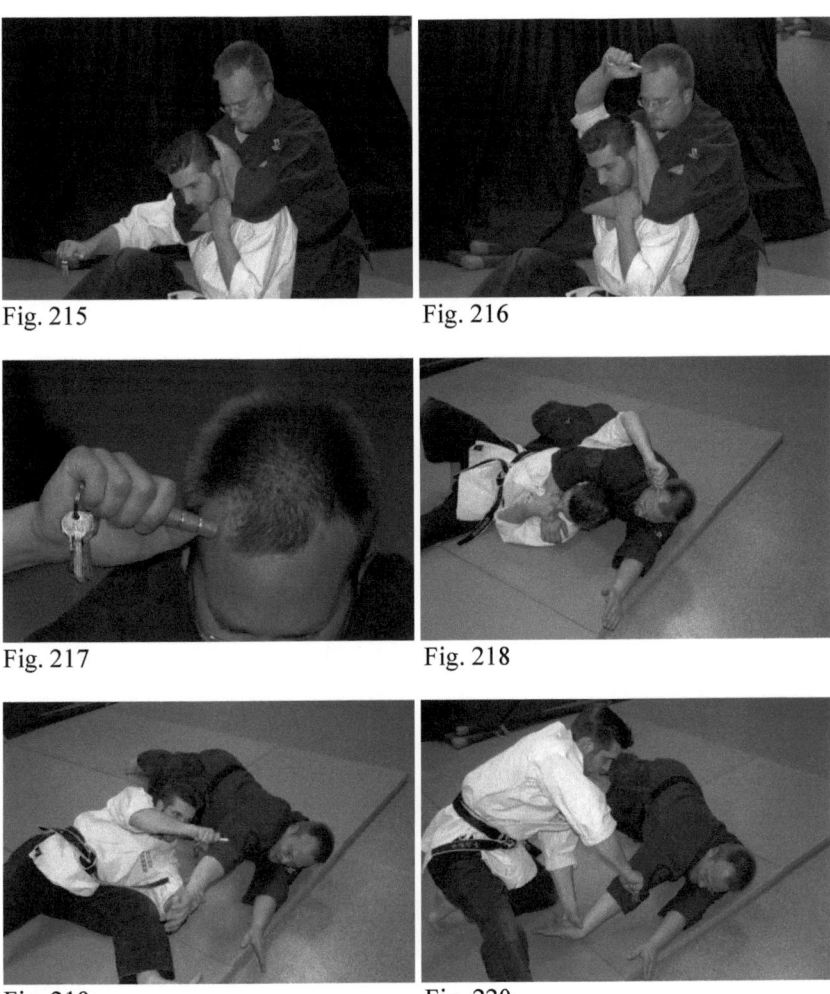

Fig. 215   Fig. 216

Fig. 217   Fig. 218

Fig. 219   Fig. 220

The defender is choked from the back while sitting down. He loosens the grip with his left hand and quickly tucks his chin in to protect himself from being choked. The he jabs the tip of the Mini Stick into his attacker's head to free himself (Fig. 215-217). The opponent falls to the side, pulling the defender with him. But he positions the Mini Stick on the elbow (Fig. 218 – 219) and puts the attacker in an arm hold. This way he can be controlled on the ground (Fig. 220).

3. Defense against kicks while sitting

Fig. 221

Fig. 222

Fig. 223

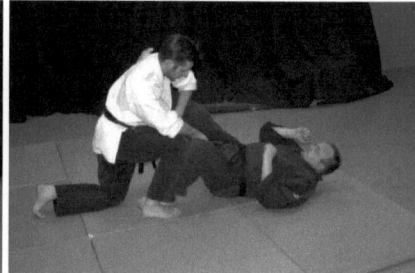

Fig. 224

Fig. 225

The defender is sitting in the zazen (seated meditation) position. The opponent attacks with a low kick from the front. Now the defender moves forward and positions his arms in a way that lets him derive the kick (Fig. 221-222). Then he jabs the Mini Stick into the attacker's genitals (Fig. 223), making him fall to the ground (Fig. 224). Now the defender is standing between his legs and has complete control. It is possible to kick into the genitals again if necessary (Fig. 225).

4. Defenses in a prone position

Fig. 226

Fig. 227

Fig. 228

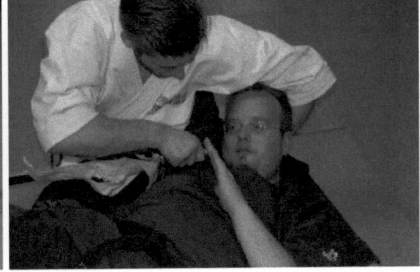

Fig. 229

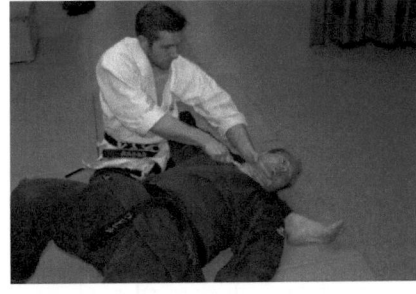

Fig. 230

The defender is lying on his belly while the attacker puts pressure on the neck and shoulders from behind (Fig. 226). Now the defender turns left while raising his left arm and jabbing the tip of the Mini Stick into the ribs (Fig. 227 – 228). He keeps turning until the attacker is brought into a supine position and stands up to gain control by applying pressure with the Mini Stick on the neck of the attacker (Fig. 229 – 230). Now a leg scissor or other ground techniques are possible.

5. Defense against leg scissors

Fig. 231

Fig. 232

Fig. 233

Fig. 234

Fig. 235

The defender is placed in leg scissors by his attacker (Fig. 231). The Mini Stick is held in the right hand with the tip near the pinky. The defender presses the tip of the Mini Stick into the tendons of the adductor muscles in the inner upper thigh to release himself from the leg scissors. At the same time he applies pressure onto the neck or collar bone (Fig. 232). The defender can press his shin onto the opponent's upper thigh for extra security. The Mini Stick is placed on the elbow and the opponent is placed in an arm hold (Fig. 233-234). This way the attacker can be controlled and brought to the ground (Fig. 235).

6. Defense against choke holds on the ground

Fig. 236

Fig. 237

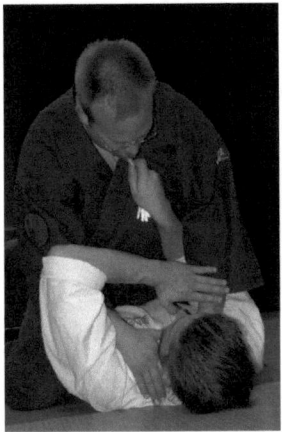

Fig. 238

The attacker sits on the defender and chokes him (Fig. 236). The defender uses his left hand to keep his opponent's hands in place while tucking his chin in. He positions the Mini Stick tip first on his attacker's neck (Fig. 237-238). Then he applies pressure on the neck and moves his hips until the opponent falls off to the left (Fig. 239). The attacker is immobilized by a kick in the ribs (Fig. 240).

Fig. 239

Fig. 240

7. Defense against headlocks while on the belly

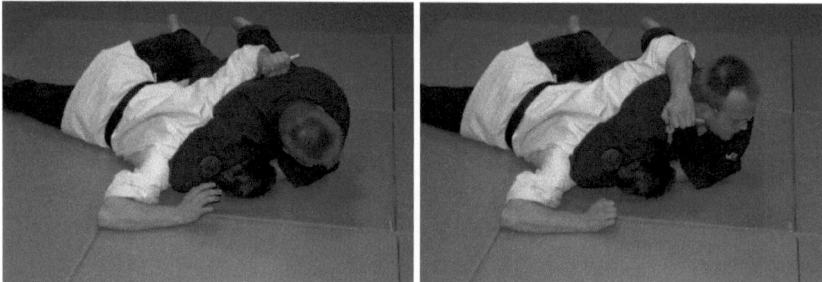

Fig. 241   Fig. 242

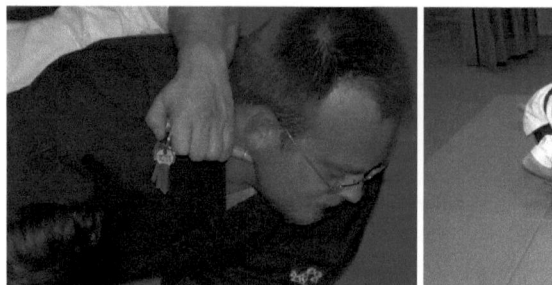

Fig. 243   Fig. 244

Fig. 245   Fig. 246

The defender is held in a headlock (Fig. 241). He positions the Mini Stick tip first behind his attacker's ear (Fig. 242-243) while simultaneously grabbing his right wrist. By applying pressure behind the attacker's ear the defender can free himself from the headlock, but still presses the opponent on the ground by controlling his left arm and shoulder (Fig. 244-245). He twists his attacker's arm so the elbow is facing upwards and puts pressure on it with his knee (Fig. 246).

8. Defense against armlock

Fig. 247

Fig. 248

Fig. 249

Fig. 250

Fig. 251

The attacker holds the opponent in a cross armlock, commonly known as a juji gatame, but without properly closing his legs (Fig. 247). The defender strongly presses the Mini Stick into the upper inner thigh of his opponent, then frees his arm out of the hold and turns towards his attacker (Fig. 248-249). The Mini Stick is passed from the left into the right hand and then thrust into the genitals of the opponent (Fig. 250). Then the defender pushes him away with his legs (Fig 251).

9. Defense against headlock whilst on the ground

Fig. 252   Fig. 253

Fig. 254   Fig. 255

The defender is held in a headlock on the ground. His left hand is free and he holds the Mini Stick with the tip near his thumb (Fig. 252). With a powerful thrust he shoves the Mini Stick into the back of his opponent (Fig. 253). Following targets are preferred: the spine, shoulder blades, muscles, between the shoulder blades, shoulder bone, latissimus, ribs and the cervical vertebrae (only apply pressure, don't thrust!). The opponent jolts his head back up because of the pain that is inflicted. The defender uses this opportunity to bring his leg back and in front of the attacker's throat, while simultaneously positioning the Mini Stick at his temple (Fig. 254). As soon as his rival is brought to the ground he places him in leg scissors and an arm tackle, and positions the Mini Stick at the opponent's larynx for complete control (Fig. 255).

Acknowledgement:

I would like to express my gratitude to Markus Wandscher who helped me by posing for the pictures as my partner; Ariane Bukowski who took the photos; Christian Gottberg who critically looked through my book; and my parents and siblings who always supported and encouraged me to find my own path against all odds.

References:

1) Mark Wiley (1994), "Filipino Martial Arts", Charles E. Tuttle Company.

2) Ernesto A. Presas (1988), "Arnis – Presas Style and Balisong", Ernesto Presas.

3) Jeff Imada (1986), "The advanced Balisong Manual", Unique Publications.

4) Masaaki Hatsumi (1981), "Stickfighting", Kodansha International.

5) Wedding / Claussen (2000), "Der Mehrzweckeinsatzstock MES / Tonfa" ["The Multipurpose MES / Tonfa Stick"], Boorberg Verlag [Boorberg Publishers].

6) Edmond Vary (1924), "Die Kunst der Selbstwehr" ["The Art of Self-Defense"], Grethlein & Co GmbH.

7) R.J. Krutwig (1991), "Ju Jitsu", Humboldt.

8) G. Siebert (1997), "Arnis – Escrima – Kali", Weinmann.